Celebration

Heaven's Rewards Show

Patti Jo Hogan-Hostettler

inCahoots LITERARY
Nashville, Tennessee

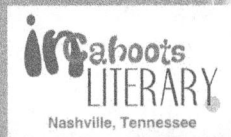

© Patti Jo Hogan-Hostettler 2016. All rights reserved.

No part of this book may be reproduced in any form or by any means without permission in writing from the publisher, except for the inclusion of brief quotations in a review.

Published by InCahoots Literary
a division of InCahoots Film Entertainment LLC
P. O. Box 111510
Nashville, TN 37222

www.incahootsliterary.com
www.incahootsfilmentertainment.com

Book design and cover photography by Michael Allen of InCahoots Literary

ISBN 978-0-9887241-7-4

Dedication

To my Heavenly Father, from whom all blessings flow. I want to thank Him for His son, Jesus Christ and for telling me to "write the book!"

And it shall come to pass that everyone who calls upon the name of the Lord shall be saved. – Acts 2:21

Contents

Acknowledgements – ix

Introduction – xi

Chapter 1 – 1

Chapter 2 – 3

Chapter 3 – 7

Chapter 4 – 11

Chapter 5 – 13

Chapter 6 – 15

Chapter 7 – 19

Chapter 8 – 23

Chapter 9 – 27

Chapter 10 – 31

Chapter 11 – 33

Chapter 12 – 39

Epilogue – 41

    My Homeless Ministry – 43

    Bible Characters – 45

About Patti Jo Hogan-Hostettler – 47

Acknowledgements

Pastor Paul Baggett ("The Happy Pastor") – thank you for being my spiritual father here on earth. You lived the teachings of Jesus, and now you are celebrating with the Lord from on high. You are truly missed by all.

Denise Thomas – for being my true friend, believing in *Celebration* and for working so hard with the homeless ministry. You are a blessing to all who know you!

Robin Hardin – for giving me the encouragement to write *Celebration*. Please read Robin's book, *Walking, Talking, Debating, and Arguing with God*. You find it on Amazon. Robin, you are an amazing woman!

Cravin and Nyle Hogan – my sons who I love with every being of my body. You lost your father at a very young age but through it all, God has and will always watch over you. Life is not easy and is not fair, read your Bible, seek His help, and all will be well.

Joe Hostettler, Sr. – thank you for putting up with me!

G. Michael Allen – thank you for being my publisher. I couldn't have done this book without you.

Introduction

Celebration came about because of a Wednesday night service at Pastor Paul Baggett's church, Living To Go Life Center, in Nashville, Tennessee. Visiting from Michigan was guest speaker Pastor Baker. This pastor was on fire, prophesying to all of us. My friends and I were sitting towards the back when Pastor Baker came around saying, "Write the book! God says, 'Write the book!'" I knew he was talking to me. Later in the service this man of God walked toward us and called us up front. "Hurry," he said, "This can't wait." He prophesied with each of us. He remarked to me that God told him I was an observer and needed to change because God has a lot of work for me. He also said God wanted me to put a pen and paper at my bedside this night. Pastor Baker said, "I don't know why, but you do this." Then he blessed me.

Later that night in the bedroom I placed pen and paper on my side of the bed. Then I dropped to my knees and asked God to let me know what I'm supposed to do. I got into bed and went to sleep. At 2:21 a. m. I was awakened from a deep sleep with a thunder in my whole being and this word repeating many times: CELEBRATION, CELEBRATION, CELEBRATION. This booming sound was resonating from inside a big metal barrel. I picked up my pen and paper and began writing *Celebration*.

Before that Wednesday night service, I worked the *CMT Music Video Awards Show*. My job was escorting artists down the red carpet. As people were screaming and cameras flashing at these worldly people, all of a sudden, I had a thought. I told a friend as we waited for the next artist to arrive, "Wouldn't it be great if this was an awards show from heaven? You know, instead of famous people getting out of the limos, Biblical people like Moses, Paul and yes, Jesus would be arriving. And we would walk them down the red carpet and into a show of their own."

I testify God gave me this idea. God told me to write the book! God blessed me with the name of this book.

I know you will enjoy reading this wonderful *Celebration*. I'm looking forward to the celebration when Jesus comes back. That's one celebration we don't want to miss.

I give all the glory to our God in heaven and give great thanks in the Mighty Name of Jesus Christ. Amen.

1

It's nighttime in the world famous Music City USA, also known as Nashville, Tennessee. More than 100 big searchlights light the perimeter of the city. A celebration is about to begin. All the parking lots across the city are filled to the max. Police officers are directing traffic. The streets are alive with activity. On every street corner vendors and food trucks are selling refreshments. Everyone is in awe with the feeling of excitement that is here, and it is making them all thirst and hunger. And for what? They can't explain.

At every newspaper stand the headlines read: **CELEBRATION!!!**

A camera follows a woman walking backstage at a big stadium. Groups of volunteers have arrived and are excited to be there. They are given instructions on what to do. A group of people are standing in a circle holding hands and praying for a "good show."

Many rooms at this venue are filled with busy workers. One room has people going over the scripts one more time. Make-up rooms are a flutter. The best hair and make-up artists are anxious and ready for the guests to arrive.

Food is set up in another room down the hall. The homeless, the widows, the drug addicts, and the alcoholics—the misfits that society has shunned—are waiting in line. They are happy to be eating and inside – away from the elements of the weather. They don't have a clue about this show. They aren't aware their lives are about to change.

Out front, TV crews are set up on one of the most prestigious and all important red carpet they have ever hoped to be on. Some are doing live telecasts. Some will take their interviews and edit them together.

The great thing about this show is NO ONE PERSON is aware of who will be walking down the red carpet and what this CELEBRATION is. Everyone believes the show guests arriving tonight are rock stars, movie stars and celebrities that will hand out and accept trophies for achievement in each of their fields of entertainment.

The crowd outside is gathered across from the red carpet and will try to get a glimpse of who will be arriving at the show. They hold up signs reading: We Love You, You're The Best, and You Got Our Vote.

2

On Highway 31W, truckers are coming and going slowly. This highway was constructed in the 1920s and was the only highway connecting southern Alabama to northern Michigan. It was a route taken by numerous country and bluegrass artists and anyone with big dreams wanting to make a living in Music City USA.

Traffic wouldn't be coming down this two lane highway tonight if it wasn't for a three-car accident on Interstate 65. This stretch of interstate has a pretty bad curve coming down the ridge from White House, Tennessee, to Nashville, right before you get to Millersville. It's all downhill, and the truckers have a hard time keeping their rigs in their own lanes. At this point on the big road a billboard reads, "Are you ready to meet the Lord?" It was probably put there years ago due to all the accidents.

Again, that bad curve was a part of the accident. A big 18-wheeler was coming down the ridge way too fast and collided right on that curve with a couple of automobiles. Helicopters were brought in to take the victims into Nashville. Thankfully, everyone will be okay, except for the frustrated ones stuck on the closed-down interstate and re-routed to the two-lane alternate, Highway 31W.

A hitch-hiker, Daniel Adams, decided to hike over to the alternate route. He wasn't in any hurry to get anywhere, but figured he'd catch a ride with one of the truckers who heard about the accident and had already made it out of the stalled traffic.

Daniel was a really bad guy who drifted from town-to-town. He came from the typical broken family. His mama was serving time in prison when she had him, and his daddy moved to Nashville to pursue his wild dream of becoming a big country star. They say it's always good to follow your dreams. Unfortunately for Daniel's dad, his dream only happened when he was sober enough to remember.

So, in the mean time, Daniel was shifted between family members who would try to love him and show him a happy home. Heck, the *Serenity Prayer* was on all of their walls. They tried, and they tried, but their prayers and all their patience together couldn't break into his cold heart. Daniel was so uncontrollable. He went from foster home to foster home. Heaven knows they tried. No one could handle him. Daniel would steal, lie and hang out with the roughest people in town. They would drink, smoke and do any kind of drugs they could get their hands on.

Daniel had all kinds of tattoos. His hair was getting pretty thin. You could see in his eyes how tired he was. He was tired of running. He was tired of stealing. He was tired of life. If Daniel could only settle down. All the girls he has ever known were worse off than him. The sheriff in the last town told him if he was still there come morning, he was going to jail.

So now, Daniel was going to another city. Only this time he was going to Nashville. That's the last place he heard his daddy was. He was gonna look him up and find out why he left him before he was even born. Daniel would ask his grandma questions about his dad, but they would always go unanswered.

His mother was dead from a drug overdose, his praying grandma who loved him more than life itself was gone, and the rest of the family didn't want anything to do with him. So, Daniel decided to go and get answers in person. What did he have to lose, if his daddy was still alive and in Nashville.

Daniel, on the shoulder of the road, flagged down a truck in the slow-moving heavy traffic.

"Where you headed?" asked Willie, the truck driver.

"Nashville," replied Daniel.

Willie motioned Daniel to hop on up and remarked, "I'll be going right through Nashville. Heading for Alabama myself. Got to get these pigs down there to the stockyard. Hey, have you heard about the big show tonight in Nashville? It's being advertised between every other song on this radio station. The truckers on the cb radio are talking about parking down there and trying to find out what all the fuss is about. No one knows what it is, or who'll be there. It's a big secret. Some sort of celebration. Anyways, with all this traffic we should be there in a couple of hours."

"Nope, I haven't heard a thing about any show," said Daniel, "I'm going there to find my Dad." That was all Daniel remembered saying before he fell asleep.

In Nashville things were really stirring up. Everything was in place at the stadium. People could feel something was about to happen.

The stadium stage looked like it was decorated by angels from heaven. This was basically the theme and the feeling set designers were wanting everyone to feel. Beautiful blue backdrops. White fluffy clouds hanging. Beautiful columns around the whole stage. A gigantic crystal chandelier hung from the center of what looked like heaven. The podium looked like a chariot made out of gold. Hanging in the air was a beautiful scent that no one could figure out. Hanging on the walls were beautiful red, white and purple drapes. The clock was ticking down the seconds until show time.

3

"Hey son," said Willie, the pig haulin' truck driver, "It's time to get up. We're just about to Nashville."

"Goodness gracious!" said Daniel as he opened his eyes. "Look at all those lights! What in the world is happening?"

"That must be that Celebration show extravaganza everyone's talking about," declared Willie. "It beats me what's happening. But I'll tell you what, that thing has got my curiosity up. I'm pulling into this truck stop to find out what all the hoopla is. I've never in my sixty four years seen or felt this way about anything."

As Willie pulled into the truck stop, Daniel jumped out of the cab saying, "There ain't nothing good ever happens. I'm sure this whole trip has been a waste of time for me. Thanks a lot, man. You wouldn't happen to know where there's a mission in town do ya?"

"Nope, sure don't," remarked Willie, "Come inside and we can ask around." By the time Willie circled his truck to check his pigs, Daniel was gone. Willie just shrugged and proceeded to call his wife to let her know what he was doing in Nashville.

Daniel was in a bad part of town where most truck stops were, but to him it was just another dirty town. Prostitutes and drug addicts were hanging out under the bridge he was walking past. "Hey," said this scraggy lookin' character, "You got any change?"

Daniel looked him straight in the eyes and barked, "Do I look like I have any change?" That's when two other guys came up behind Daniel and beat the crap out of him. He was just about to pass out when a man with gentle-looking eyes reached down to help him up. "Oh thanks, man," Daniel exclaimed, "I thought I was a goner." The man had long hair, a beard and a gentle voice to go along with his gentle eyes.

"You look like you could use a hot meal. Come, follow me," said the stranger. Daniel straightened up the best he could – fixing his shirt and knocking the dirt off his pants. Daniel asks the stranger, "Where are we going? What's your handle?"

The stranger remarks in a gentle tone, "Daniel, you're not going to believe this, but, what I'm saying is the truth. You came here to Nashville to find your dad. You've had an empty feeling in your soul for as long as you can remember. Tonight is your night."

Daniel started backing up and had this wild glare in his eyes. "How did you know my name was Daniel? How do you know what only I can feel? Daniel thinks,

I must have hit my head on that concrete back there. I must be passed out and in a coma.

"Listen mister," said Daniel, "ummmm, thanks for everything. I'll catch you on the flip side."

Daniel started walking quickly up the street towards all the lights. "Daniel," the stranger called out, "I have peace without end for you. Please, give me a chance. I'm here to help you. Let's go get that hot meal and talk."

"Well," Daniel said, "I am pretty hungry. Hey man, what's with all these limos?"

"These limos are carrying great men and women," said the stranger. "They are heading for the red carpet. Come, let's hurry."

4

In the stadium, things are coming together. Scripts are finished, people are in their places, and the audience is being led to their seats. Someone is knocking at the side door. It is Daniel and his new friend he's still not sure about. The gentle stranger asks if food is still being served. A staff member reports, "They are back there cleaning up, but I'm sure they'll find you something to eat."

Daniel is still thinking he is lying in a coma somewhere. As they walk into the room with food, Daniel looks around with amazement. The room is full of homeless, down on their luck people. Daniel declares, "What's going on here? This big fancy place with china, cloth napkins and silverware is being used to serve these people? Don't they know there won't be any silverware left?" Then Daniel chuckles, "You better check pockets before they leave."

As Daniel is seated and begins to eat, he hears rehearsals of some sort – sounds like a man singing with just his guitar. "Hey," Daniel states, "That dude's pretty good. This ain't such a bad place after all." Daniel looks for his new friend, but he is nowhere to be found. The lights blink on and off, and a lady holding a clip board and walkie-talkie enters the room. She announces on her walkie, "I believe all our guests have arrived and eaten. I'm taking them to their seats."

Daniel gets up to leave because he, like the others, is clueless to what is happening and have never been treated like royalty before in his life. He's looking for a exit. Daniel murmurs, "This is just too weird. Could it be all those drugs coming and messing with my head? I must have really been beaten up bad under that bridge." For Daniel and the others, there is no way out. They are led to their VIP seats in front of the stage.

On the red carpet, the media is everywhere by now. This is such a phenomena. All TV stations are breaking into their telecasts and are now going out as live broadcasts, even TBN and CBN are there. The street across from the red carpet is full to the max. Policemen line the red carpet. They believe this event could turn into a riot at any moment.

Volunteers are standing at the start of the red carpet while the stage manager with a headset is talking to someone. "We're ready here," states the headset man, "All is in place and ready to go. Who do we have arriving first?"

5

Cameras, Lights, Action!

A stretch limousine pulls up to the red carpet. All eyes are on the door as the chauffeur wearing all white comes around to open the door. There is dead silence around the whole city and could be around the whole world as far as anyone knows. It's so quite you can hear a pin drop. As the door opens, that scent hits the air – the same scent in the stadium. It has the smell of perfume. This scent of spikenard fills the air. It was taken from pink blossomed plants in the Himalayan Mountains of northern India. Just then a woman exits the limo carrying an alabaster jar filled with spikenard.

A reporter comes up to the woman and asks, "Who are you? What is this celebration about? People all over are asking and watching."

She answers, "I am the woman who poured my perfume on Jesus' head. Jesus said I did an excellent thing for him. I did the only thing I could do for him. And because of this, Jesus said wherever the Good News is preached in all the world, what I had done will be told, and people will remember me."

The reporter's mouth falls open! The cameraman is stunned and can't move! The woman starts walking down the red carpet towards the stage. The frenzy across the street has died down. Now, instead of screaming, people are falling to their knees as this woman passes by. As cameras are recording her movement down the aisle, reporters are talking in low voices as if they were reporting a televised golf game.

In the stadium, everyone is seated and are aware of the silence outside. There is a reverent feeling. The orchestra starts playing, and Alvin Slaughter sings, "Holy Spirit Rain Down."

6

Another stretch limo arrives. Cameras are once again flashing. Only now people are realizing this is a blessed event. All are thirsty. The volunteers also realize the blessing bestowed on them and to be privileged enough to walk these guests down the red carpet and into the stage area. As the door of the limo opens, everyone is curious who could be next. In the crowd, people are speculating and hoping for their favorite person to exit. All is quiet as Paul steps forth and walks onto the red carpet.

Paul stops and speaks, "I am Paul. You might know me from the Book of Acts. I am a Jew. I arrested men and women. I persecuted the people who followed the way of Jesus. Some of them were even killed. I was on my way to arrest and punish believers when a bright light from heaven suddenly flashed all around me. I was on the road to Damascus when this happened. I fell to the ground and heard a voice saying, 'Why are you persecuting me?' This was the voice of Jesus. I am here to witness to all. Be baptized and wash your sins away.

Trust in Jesus to save you. Go tell the world or even your closest friend that Jesus lives and God has a plan for each one of us. Believe and be saved!" Paul then waves to the crowd and heads toward the stage.

Cameras begin flashing, and reporters continue their live coverage.

A well-known Nashville reporter, Roxane, is standing on the red carpet. Anyone who is anyone in Nashville knows that when Roxane is covering an event, everyone listens, because she is known to get to the bottom of everything she reports. She talks into the camera, "This is some show down here. I have never seen such an event. I understand from the folks back at the station that we are witnessing first hand a show that the whole world is watching. Folks – the feelings down here are incredible. There is such peace. People are praising the Lord on every street corner. This is surely a sight to behold." Roxane grabs her earpiece and listens for a second. She looks up at the camera with a confused look on her face.

"I'm getting conflicting reports the President of the United States is on his way. Air Force One is reported landing at Nashville International as we speak! Now back to you."

Back at the studio, they call in all personnel. This event is on every satellite in every country in the world.

In the stadium, in-house monitors are showing what is going on down on the red carpet. Limo after limo are arriving. Each one is carrying special guests. The camera zooms onto the red carpet. Arriving at this time is Max Lucado, Martin Luther King, Norman Vincent Peale, and Mother Teresa. You can see and hear the crowd cheering and taking pictures. Each guest is waving to all.

7

People are gathering at the stadium. All total so far, 880,000 in the stadium and surrounding area. There are people coming from all over. Now, everyone on the face of the earth knows of this Celebration.

As another beautiful white limo arrives, the stage manager, Billy T., is being interviewed by a TV crew from Kenya. Their first question is, "Were you aware of what your job was going to entail tonight?"

Billy T, answers, "I was told to report here and take care of the show guests arriving and make sure they walk the red carpet."

Their second question is, "Did you know at any time what kind of show was taking place tonight?" Billy T. scratches his head and answers, "As a matter of fact, I was in the shower this morning, and a premonition came to me. Something told me to be prepared for a celebration, but, no, I didn't know such dignitaries would be arriving. I'm just thankful I'm a Christian. I gave my life to Jesus when I was eight years old."

TV crew asks their last question before the next guest arrives. "Are you hoping that when you open one of these limos that the big man himself will step out? You know, Jesus."

Billy T. raises both his hands towards heaven and yells, "Praise God. Hallelujah!" He jumps up and down and in a circle. "All will go to their knees if he shows up! Glory to God!"

Just then, another limo pulls up, and the other stage manager, Russell, leans into the limo to ask who exactly has arrived before he announces it to the crowd. Russell proudly turns to the cameras and the crowd and says, "Everyone, please, welcome Nimrod!" Once again, the crowd across the street are cheering and praying.

Nimrod exits the limo and walks halfway down the red carpet. He is handed a microphone and speaks, "Greetings! Some of you might not know me, because you would have to read Genesis to know who I am. And I know, in today's lifestyle, Genesis is not a top priority. You could take a little time each day and read Genesis a little bit at a time. It wouldn't hurt. Anyway, I am very proud to be part of this glorious Celebration. I am one of Cush's descendents. I was a heroic warrior. I was a mighty hunter in the Lord's sight. I was the one who built the foundation for His, (he raises his hands towards heaven), empire in the land of Babylonia. My families were the families that came from Noah's sons."

Nimrod turns to the stage manager and asks, "Has Noah arrived yet?" He turns back to the crowd and continues, "Listen, I'm telling you all, read your Bibles. I'm in Genesis. You won't regret it." Nimrod hands the microphone back to the stage manager and continues to walk the red carpet toward the stage area.

8

The stage is full of Praise dancers. They are dancing to a beautiful tune and wearing beautiful outfits. The production is second to none. Smoke fills the stage floor, and some dancers are running back and forth with beautiful flags of every color.

Then, out come mimes – doing a beautiful mime. The feeling in the stadium is calmness. The homeless in the VIP seats are in amazement. They cannot believe what is taking place – thinking they were just coming for food. They realize not only have their bodies been fed, but now they are being fed spiritually. The homeless are loving this Celebration.

Another stretch limousine arrives. As the cameras are flashing, the spectators wonder who the next exalted great will be. The limo door opens, and King David steps out. He waves to everyone across the street and heads down the red carpet until he reaches the microphone stand. He proudly proclaims his story. "After my victory over Goliath, and many more battles after that, I was made King David. I was only thirty years old when this all happened. I ruled over Israel for forty years. That's the reason it is called, City of David."

Across the street, young children are sitting on the ground with their moms, dads, grandmas, and grandpas. They are listening as David continues with his story. "When I was made King, we feasted for three days! To show you how it was back in those days, I have brought to this Celebration a vast supply of flour, fig cakes, raisins, wine, olive oil, cattle, and sheep. Enjoy!"

David turns around and claps his hands two times. Coming down the red carpet are servant men and women carrying these supplies and hands them out to the people around the red carpet. As music is playing, David tells the people, "I also wrote a Song of Praise: 'Give thanks to the Lord, for He is good! His faithful love endures forever!'" Everyone shouts "Amen" and "praise the Lord." David continues on to the stage area.

What a great night in Nashville, Tennessee! Pulling up in the next limo are Barnabas and Daniel. Barnabas is handed a microphone and when he speaks, all listen, "Good Evening Ladies and Gentlemen! Isn't it great to be alive! I am Barnabas. I'm known as the great encourager. I encouraged John Mark. I helped him to become a great leader in the church. Listen to me, everything that was written in the past was written to teach us. The scriptures give us patience and encouragement. Get your Bibles out and start reading your scriptures! Here's an encouragement to my dear friend, Robin Hardin, 'Continue to encourage one another.'"

Barnabas hands the microphone to Daniel and walks toward his seat in the stadium.

Cameras from rooftops zoom into newly arriving guests coming out of the limo. They are Matthew, Mark, Luke, John, and Matthias.

They stop halfway down the red carpet for a photo shoot. You can see the excitement in their eyes for the show is about to begin.

Daniel thanks Barnabas and continues speaking to the people. Standing on each side of Daniel are two beautiful lions, clearly under his control, Daniel says, "We need to find courage to stand against pressures and to not compromise our beliefs. They pressured me so badly. They wanted me to set aside my faith and worship a king! I wouldn't, and I didn't! I was sent to die in a den of lions! But God's power protected me! Through everything, I remained faithful to God. HE IS IN CONTROL. My message to all tonight is this: when things get rough (both lions stand on their hind legs and give a loud roar) and believe me," Daniel says, "they do get rough, and when you are under pressure from every side, know that God is working to protect his people. Rely on God, and remain faithful to Him, no matter what happens."

The crowd is just ecstatic. With this, Daniel and his two large lions take a bow and continue toward the stage area.

9

As the Celebration is about to begin, another scene is happening on the banks of the Cumberland River. A bad evil vibe is coming up the river. You can feel the presence of sadness, hurt and agony. Sitting there is a homeless man named, Cowboy. He is well-known in the homeless community and makes his home on the banks of the river.

Cowboy is looking up towards the city and wonders what has everybody and his brother yelling and shouting. Something is happening tonight that can't be seen by the human eye. There is a battle raging between good and evil. I guess you could say Cowboy was at the wrong place and definitely at the wrong time. He is just minding his own business when a woman starts screaming at the top of her lungs, "He's gonna kill me! Oh God, please, the crazy maniac is gonna kill me!" Running in this woman's tracks is a crazed man. In his hand you can see the light reflecting off of something shiny.

The crazed man is yelling something about not caring about any Celebration and all those goody two shoes up there hoopin' and hollerin' – praising some silly invisible man they call Jesus! This crazed man claims he is working for Big S – Satan! He looks at Cowboy with an evil look in his eyes. "Get out of my way Cowboy, or this knife will have your name on it! You're just like all the rest of them with their pretty clothes on carrying that stupid book they call the Bible. Going around quoting it all day long! Well, I'm sick of this! Here, I'll quote cha somethin' out of that Bible! An eye for an eye and a tooth for a tooth! Now, I come for my revenge. This woman did me wrong and now she's gonna die!"

Just then the man steps forward to stab the woman in her chest. But Cowboy lunges forward to grab the knife out of the man's hand. When he does, the knife pierces Cowboy's heart. This evil crazed person starts laughing and quoting passages from the Bible. Looking down at Cowboy laying on the ground he says, "Go get one of those people celebrating Jesus up there and see if he can heal you!" His course voice sounds so evil.

This crazy man lunges toward the woman and knocks her out. Thinking she was dead, he runs off laughing. As the woman lays knocked out, a man comes to her. He blesses her and tells her to get up. She wakes up not knowing what happened. This man with long hair, a gentle voice and beautiful gentle eyes finds the crazy man and rebukes him. He says, "This night is a night of Celebration, and no one under the sun is going to ruin it for the people who love God."

The crazy man falls to the ground in a fetal position and starts throwing up, cursing God and everything on earth. The gentle man lays his hands on this crazed idiot, and the tide turns. The crazy man is now calm and sorry for what he had done to Cowboy. "Cowboy is at peace now," says the gentle stranger, "He has gone home to be with his Father in Heaven. His work on earth is done." They both get up and start walking up the hill towards the Celebration.

On the ground lay Cowboy. The story about Cowboy is every Saturday he would go up from the river to eat and visit with that church that brought food to the hungry and prayed for the needy. Cowboy knew Jesus and accepted Him into his heart. During Cowboy's last breath he prays, "My Father, who art in heaven," raising his hand upward, "I'm ready to go."

Early the next morning his body will be discovered with his hands clasped around the small Bible given to him by those Christian servants of God that help the needy.

10

Everyone is waiting with great expectation of what will happen next. Lights all over the city are shut down. Complete darkness. Complete silence. There is a great big thundering, and then it all happens. The ceiling opens up, and all eyes are turned towards heaven. Out of the sky come hundreds of doves. Slowly, the lights reappear on stage.

None other than Moses, himself, makes his way up to the podium and in a soft voice says, "Let us pray. Oh God in heaven, let everyone who hears the message tonight take it in through their hearts and all the way to their souls. Let us all proclaim you Lord of Lords. Let the show begin! And with this we say, in Jesus name, Amen!" Then Moses makes his way backstage.

Smoke fills the stage and a distant sound of drums come into the stadium. Coming in from both sides of the stage are the most beautifully decorated Native American Indians – dancing for the Lord, singing to the Lord and praising our God in Heaven. It is the most beautiful pageantry anyone has ever witnessed and goes on for nearly an hour with no one complaining. As they leave the stage, the lights go dim once more.

All of a sudden a voice is heard, "Clap your hands children!" Appearing on stage is Bryan Duncan singing his song "Holy Rollin'." The audience is up on their feet, clapping and singing to this upbeat spiritual song. Even the homeless in the VIP section are clapping, singing and dancing with happiness.

Daniel, in particular, is observing everything and is thinking he isn't worthy of the feelings he has. He can't explain these feelings coming from way deep inside of him.

These new feelings started when that gentle man under the bridge helped him. Daniel kept thinking about what he had said – "Tonight is your night." What was he talking about? Daniel starts weeping, just standing there, crying like a baby.

11

As Bryan Duncan finished his show, Moses comes out and introduces his next guest, "Glory be to God! Isn't this wonderful! I want everyone to put your hands together and welcome one of my brethrens I love dearly. Please welcome to the stage, Amos!"

Amos comes walking onto the stage with pride, dignity and seriousness, and the audience becomes silent quickly. He grabs the microphone and says, "Greetings. I have come with a heavy heart. I have a message from heaven. Please wake up! Church and humanity get together! Pastors! Start telling us what we need to hear. Not what we want to hear. Morals! We need a revival for the Lord! We need to get on a war-footing. We are in war! In a spiritual war and we need to wake up! We need to drop to our knees. We need to pray to God and give an anointing. Pull down strong holds. Every thought needs to be in the obedience of God. It's time to take back our territory the devil has taken from us. We are on the winning side! Remember, we who love the Lord are on the winning side." Amos gets a standing ovation and exits the stage with his arms stretched out towards heaven.

Moses introduces a young man, "Please welcome Lee Adams."

The lights are dim once more. Lee Adams comes on stage carrying an acoustic guitar and a stool. It's dark except for the spotlight shining on him. Sitting on the stool Lee begins telling his story with his self-penned song, "Dear Jesus," as he plays softly on his guitar. He almost whispers, "When I was young, I didn't realize what it meant to be part of the family of God. God was the furthest thing from my mind. I loved no one. The ones who cared for me, I would hurt them any way I could. I hung with the wrong crowd. Bellying up to the bar drinking and smoking was my idea of a night of relaxation. What started out good, always ended up bad. I'd pass out who knows where and I never knew how I got to the places. I couldn't hold down a job. Things would go good for the first week or two, and I'd get my hands on a paycheck and that would be the end of that job. It got so bad for me that I found myself living on the streets. When you're living on the streets, that means everyone has given up on you. My flesh was weak, and my spirit was gone. Loneliness was a constant companion."

Daniel begins to listen to this man's story. It sounded so familiar. He was relating to everything this guy was saying.

Lee continues his story. "I got hooked up with this girl named Dorothy. Everyone called her Dottie. She had a beautiful face and beautiful eyes to match. We fell in love. Dottie happened to have this little problem. She was a crack head. She'd turn to prostitution to support her habit. I even got on the stuff before I met Jesus. I had never been lower in my life than the day Dottie told me she was pregnant with my child. Oh no, not my child I said. No way, I'm out of here. That was the night I left. I never saw her again. Never saw the child she said was mine. The last I heard, Dottie was put in prison for breaking and entering and assault with a deadly weapon. She was in prison when she gave birth to a beautiful baby boy. My blood ran cold when I heard this. I turned to alcohol to ease the pain of not knowing if I had a child on this earth. Could I have a son? I had this emptiness that would never be filled.

That was until I met this man who would come with his church every Saturday to feed the hungry. I went over to the parking lot right over there on 8th Avenue for months. Those people were kind and always had the best food. While they were feeding us, a few of them would start singing old gospel hymns. This black man named Fred would join in and sometimes bring his harmonica along. The preacher, who everyone called 'The Happy Pastor,' would jump on the back of a pick up truck and preach to us.

He would always ask is there someone out there that wants Jesus? Raise your hand if you want Jesus. Raise your hand if you want someone to pray with you.

I'll never forget that Saturday when I raised my hand. I found Jesus in that parking lot. After that, they would come and pick me up on Sunday mornings, and I would go to church.

The night I was baptized, Pastor Paul proclaimed, 'Son, I baptize you in the name of the Father, the Son and the Holy Ghost!' Down into the water I went and came out of that water filled with the Holy Ghost! To this day, I pray everyday for a miracle to happen in my life. Someday, I know, God is going to bring my son to me, and my life will be complete."

There wasn't a dry eye in the place. The Spirit of the Lord was present.

Just then a voice calls out from the VIP seating. A searching spotlight finds Daniel as he stands face-to-face with Lee. They lock eyes. Tears weld up as Daniel speaks, "Are you my father?"

"Son?" Lee asks.

Daniel runs and jumps up on the stage. It's obvious that father and son have met for the first time. There is no question about it. The two look like "two peas in a pod." Father and son embrace as the music starts up, and the Celebration continues.

An announcement is made during altar call for anyone wanting to be baptized can go to the side of the stage where John the Baptist is baptizing all who want to accept Jesus into their lives.

Daniel walks with his father over to that side of the stage and John the Baptist asks, "Daniel, do you want Jesus in your life?"

"Yes I do," Daniel says and goes into the water and is baptized. Oh Happy Day! Daniel comes out of that water praising God and thanking him for getting his father and him together. Daniel exclaims, "Family, that's what we are. I love you Dad."

"I love you, Daniel," exclaims Lee Adams.

That night not only was Daniel baptized, but over 880,000 people were baptized throughout the night and the next few days. A celebration was had by all.

As the music was playing, people were praise dancing, and souls were being saved.

Big screens hung everywhere in the venue displaying scriptures from Esther 9:22, Isaiah 61:3, Philippians 4:4, and 1Thessalonians 5:16-18 which reads, *"Always be Joyful. Pray continually and give thanks whatever happens. That is what God wants for you in Christ Jesus."*

12

Once again, out of nowhere, the sound of loud thunder and lightning is all around with a whirlwind making everyone's hair stand on end. Once again, no one has a clue what is happening next. All of a sudden everyone looks up.

The whole roof of the stadium is wide-open, and there in the clouds is God sitting on his throne. To his right is Jesus. They are happy with all. Everyone inside and outside bow down on their knees and praise God – thanking him for their blessings.

The roof closes back up as one more announcement is being made from the stage by Moses, "I thank each and everyone for coming to the Celebration." Moses says Jesus spoke to him, and God wanted everyone tonight to know one thing, "He knows your every need. He cares. Continue to pray to Him always."

As Daniel and his father walk down the aisle, he hears someone calling him, "Hey Boy!" Daniel sees Willie, the pig hauler. "Hey, Willie," says Daniel, "I want you to meet my dad. Willie picked me up outside of town. If it wasn't for your kindness Willie, I would never have met my dad. I want to thank you."

"Aw heck, Daniel," remarks Willie, "If it wasn't for you, I would never have stopped here tonight. Because I did, my arthritis is gone! I went up to the altar, and Jesus healed my body of all hurts."

In unison all three men say, "Praise God!" They laugh.

Daniel and his dad look up as the roof closes. Daniel sees Jesus. Jesus looks back. Daniel discovers Jesus is the gentle man that helped him under the bridge. With tear-filled eyes, Daniel tells Jesus, "Thank you." Jesus nods his head and gently smiles once again.

The Celebration continues.

Epilogue

My Homeless Ministry

It was a beautiful sunny morning when Anthony, a homeless man, looked up towards the sky and stated, "There is 880,000." He looked through his hands (like a photographer or a director looking for the perfect angle), looked at me, then back towards the sky and said, "880,000 people there." God used Anthony to let me know the number of people who attended His "Celebration."

We were a team who worked hard for our church's homeless ministry. Whoever wanted to come help us were welcomed with opened arms. On Friday nights we would pick up all the left-over pastries at Panera Bread, take it back to the church, wrap each one individually and meet again on Saturday mornings to prepare the food and drive to downtown Nashville.

We would arrive at the empty parking lot on 8th Avenue behind the main library. A line of 40-50 homeless people were always waiting for our arrival. We would jump into action, setting up tables for the food, preparing the drinks, the snacks, and the chance to fellowship and talk about Jesus. As we fed them the best hot dogs in Nashville, we would preach, sing a couple gospel songs and most importantly, pray with them.

Sometimes, our team would pool our money and buy Greyhound bus tickets to send kids home for a new start on life.

So you ask, does God communicate with us? The Bible says in John 10:27, "My sheep hear my voice, and I know them, and they follow me." I truly believe God communicates with us. He spoke to me at 2:21 a. m. about writing this book. He spoke through Anthony as the number in attendance. He gave me the characters in this book. Yes, God does communicate with us, and all we need to do is listen and obey His words.

I will forever remember our Homeless Ministry. I am so very thankful for the many times my grandchildren, Kaylee and Austin, came along, gave their time and learned first-hand how to be a blessing to those less fortunate. And for everyone else who helped, thank you. I know we have all been blessed.

Bible Characters

These Bible characters have these traits:

1. Abraham was old.
2. Jacob was insecure.
3. Leah was unattractive.
4. Joseph was abused.
5. Moses stuttered.
6. Gideon was poor.
7. Samson was codependent.
8. Rahab was immoral.
9. David had an affair and all kinds of family problems.
10. Elijah was suicidal.
11. Jeremiah was depressed.
12. Jonah was reluctant.
13. Naomi was a widow.
14. John the Baptist was eccentric to say the least.
15. Peter was impulsive and hot-tempered.
16. Martha worried a lot.
17. The Samaritan woman had several failed marriages.
18. Zacchaeus was unpopular.
19. Thomas had doubts.
20. Paul had poor health.
21. Timothy was timid.

This is quite a variety of misfits, but God used each of them in his service. He will use you, too, if you stop making excuses.

About Patti Jo Hogan-Hostettler

Patti Jo is a retired television writer/producer. Originally from Joliet, Illinois, Patti Jo, her husband Ronnie Lee Hogan and their two children, Cravin and Nyle, moved to Nashville, Tennessee, over 30 years ago. Patti Jo and Ronnie arrived in the Music City with a passion for a career in the entertainment business.

Patti Jo landed a career-making job with The Nashville Network (TNN), working in various positions from production assistant to coordinating producer, but she is most proud of her title as writer/producer for Country Music Television (CMT), an affiliate of MTV Networks.

One of her fondest career memories is when the Joliet Herald newspaper gave her recognition: hometown girl returns with the world-famous Grand Ole Opry. The Grand Ole Opry cast performed on a live television broadcast show from Joliet's beautiful Rialto Theater on June 15, 1991.

Patti Jo spends her retirement time writing short stories, traveling, and enjoying her family life with her husband, producer/director, Joe Hostettler. They reside in the Nashville, Tennessee, area.

ORDER COPIES OF THIS BOOK NOW!

NO. OF COPIES____ *Celebration* @ $12^{.95}$ each _____ x no. of copies

SUBTOTAL _____
Add 9.25 % sales tax (Tenn. residents only) _____
Postage and handling for 1st book - $3^{.75}$ _____
P & H for each additional book - $1^{.00}$ _____
TOTAL _____

ORDERED BY _____

STREET/APT NO. _____

CITY/STATE/ZIP _____

PHONE (_____)_____

Your email address: _____
We would like to send you product updates by email.

MAKE YOUR CHECK OR MONEY ORDER TO: Patti Jo Hogan-Hostettler
PLEASE MAIL THIS ORDER FORM WITH YOUR PAYMENT TO:
Patti Jo Hogan-Hostettler, P. O. Box 33, Goodlettsville, TN 37070-0033
Please allow 2 weeks for delivery. Prices are subject to change without notice.

Everyone has a story to tell.

Have you written a book?

**InCahoots Literary
could be your
PUBLISHER**

We take your manuscript, put it in book form and place your new book in the marketplace. We can also develop your promotional and marketing strategies. We love authors who will promote and sell their books in every possible way.

For more information, visit our Web site:
www.incahootsliterary.com

P. O. Box 111510, Nashville, TN 37222

 presents our latest books

  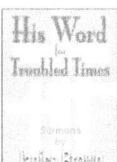   

For book information
and to order your
InCahoots Literary books
Visit
incahootsliterary.com

www.ingramcontent.com/pod-product-compliance
Lightning Source LLC
Chambersburg PA
CBHW071756040426
42446CB00012B/2585